London's 1960s Buses

a class album

John A Gray

Capital Transport

Front cover The RT family was dominant throughout the 1960s. Notwithstanding the preponderance of Routemasters in some areas for much of the decade, there were 6120 RT family vehicles in service at the start of 1960 and 3345 RTs at the end of 1969. RT 1344 is seen in Harrow Weald. *Capital Transport*

Title page After the rolling stock shortages and renewal delays experienced by London Transport during and after World War II, the ambition of nearly complete standardisation had been achieved by the onset of our period. To set the scene, Green Line RF 146, bound for distant Sussex at East Grinstead, overtakes RTL 1081 whose journey will end a few hundred yards further from Grosvenor Gardens here. *Howard Butler*

Above RT 2475 turns left from Woolwich High Street into Powis Street in March 1963 on trolleybus replacement route 96. The offside route plates on the other two RTs in view would be in use for only a further six months. *Hugh Taylor*

Facing page One-man single deckers were seen as the way forward in London Transport's mid-sixties 'Bus Reshaping Plan' but their promise proved false. At North Harrow in 1969, MBS 508 is seen new into service on RLH replacement route H1. *Capital Transport*

Back cover RTW 377 passes the National Portrait Gallery at the foot of Charing Cross Road in the summer of 1963, its extra six inches in width being unmistakable in relation to the RT. *Howard Butler*

First published 2008

ISBN 978-1-85414-319-8

Published by Capital Transport Publishing,
PO Box 250, Harrow, HA3 5ZH

Printed by CT Printing Ltd, China

The 1960s was the final decade of London's road passenger transport being run as a single entity from headquarters at 55 Broadway, Westminster. Some forty or so years later, the scene has so changed in respect to the vehicles (apart from two tiny pockets of 'heritage' operation with Routemasters) that it was felt opportune to provide this reminder of what the motor bus picture was like in the 'swinging sixties'.

Thanks for supplying the essential wherewithal go to those timely and capable photographers whose names are credited at caption ends. Any absence of credit means neither publisher nor I have been able to trace the photographer: if it's your picture, you might like to let the publisher know. Popular commercial colour photography was in its late infancy at the start of our period, but we have been able to find colour views of every class of vehicle operated by London Transport between 1960 and 1969.

The worthy books by Ken Blacker and the late Ken Glazier continue to inspire and have been consulted as valued referees. Emma Theophilus-Wright, Archivist at Transport for London's Group Archives and Records Management, gave me considerable help by unearthing minutes of various London Transport committee meetings held during the 1960s, and I thank her for all the trouble she took.

Thanks also go, alphabetically, to Lawrie Bowles, Peter Gomm, Peter Nichols, Graham Smith and Jim Whiting for their help, support and patience in my quest for accuracy; and to my wife, Sandy, for untiringly overcoming the complexities of the computer to enable the preparation of the photo captions.

John A Gray

Cambridge
January 2008

DOUBLE DECKERS

It can be observed in retrospect that London Transport, in planning for post-war passenger traffic levels, failed to recognise some of the factors that would affect decisions on the size and growth of its bus and coach fleets. Due thought had been given to replacing the remaining trams by carefully determined quantities of diesel-engined double-deck buses, and later similar preparation was made for replacing the trolleybuses between 1959 and 1962.

After wartime restrictions, Londoners, like everyone else in the country, wanted to express their new-found freedoms, and many had greater personal incomes; both factors encouraging growth in car ownership and use. Motor cycles with sidecars remained popular till the later 1950s when so-termed 'bubble cars' and cheaply made three-wheel cars gave somewhat less uncomfortable travel than the motorbike combination. A younger generation found exhilarating mobility on the newly introduced motor scooters, affordable on hire purchase terms. Many workers now preferred to use these means to travel to and from their homes and their factories.

Pre-war and through the 1940s, people had used public transport to visit friends and families or to enjoy a day out in London's countryside, at a sporting event or other attraction. Now, the bus (or Green Line coach) was gradually being forsaken for private motoring. Additionally, some of London's suburban railways were having their steam trains replaced by more attractive (and frequent) electric or diesel-powered units.

These factors combined to lower demand for bus travel, producing a need for a reduced bus fleet. Hauling London's transport infrastructure out of wartime wear, damage and neglect was no easy task, yet simultaneously, plans had to be made for the renewal of the entire fleet over a substantial period in view of the long lead times needed by under-equipped British based manufacturers to fulfil the orders.

Well before the 1960s it had become clear that too many new double-deck buses had been ordered and manufactured, even had the 1958 busmen's strike not taken place. Lasting for more than six weeks in May and June, the strike encouraged many would-be passengers to travel by other means, many not returning to bus travel. Service cuts followed. The new decade saw a surplus of perfectly serviceable RT-family buses while new Routemasters were being delivered against orders placed years earlier.

Improving service frequency was given the name 'augmenting' by London Transport management, and to outsiders may have been an unlikely consideration at a time of various obstructions in its path. Two such examples of obstruction were increasing traffic congestion which, when allowed for in service planning, could need extra buses merely to retain an established frequency rather than improving it, and the shortage of 'platform' staff – an LT term covering bus drivers and conductors.

At the start of the 1960s, with London's buses still suffering the after-effects of the six-week 1958 strike, the shortage of direct operating staff was more than ten per cent in the Central Road Services (which included trolleybuses) and just over eight per cent in the Country Bus & Coach Department. However, such shortages were not reflected in mileage lost in running the services as, with rest day and overtime working, actual mileage lost was less than one per cent. Matters deteriorated as the year progressed. By May, the figures were 13.7 per cent for central and over ten per cent for country; around ten per cent of scheduled mileage was being lost by central buses. In July, private hire activities were restricted in recognition that in view of the worsening staff position, main bus services required the priority staffing – not that this action alone would make any noticeable difference across the system. By September 1960, central was short of more than 5,000 operating staff representing nearly 16 per cent of the requirement, and country had over 600 vacancies, equivalent to nearly eleven per cent of its staffing need. Some salvation was to come at the year's end: resulting from the October pay increase, staff retention and recruitment had improved to the extent that mileage lost through staff shortage had halved between the pay award and December, down to roundly five and a half per cent. But could this figure be held, or even reduced? Time now, surely, to look into other ways of providing the travelling public with a service it needed and deserved.

In the way that the 1950s were hailed as the decade of the all-consuming RT family, then the 1960s could have been predicted as the period when the Routemaster would take on this mantle. This feeling was strengthened by the Routemaster usurping the well-liked London trolleybus, which it had begun to do in the penultimate month of 1959. It then continued replacing trolleybuses on a largely similar route pattern throughout the next two and a half years. As experience of working with the new Routemasters grew, many modifications were made, both mechanical and cosmetic, to improve the reliability, operational techniques and appearance of the type. They were found pleasant to drive, with easy-to-read controls in standardised positions which very soon became familiar. An immediate improvement noticed by drivers coming from the RT was the repositioning of the handbrake to their left, so obviating the need to avoid its RT position between doorway and seat. Conducting too was not unpleasant, despite an increase in seated capacity of eight passengers in RMs over the RT family. The vehicle's suspension was generally held to be an improvement; access along gangways was better and on a par with the RTWs. However, conducting the first new development of the established Routemaster could have been more of a handful, for with it came the increase in seats to 72: the RML had arrived. Believed to be a more economic proposition to operate than the original length version, the longer bus was in all respects the same design with an extra 2ft 4ins bay added centrally. The overall length now became a fraction under 30ft, allowed for the first time on a passenger service vehicle on two axles instead of the previous three, by a change in the regulations governing maximum sizes. A first batch of 24 was delivered over the last six months of 1961, spilling into January 1962. They were welcomed at Finchley garage as giving a better ride than the shorter version elsewhere.

With the trolleybus system now replaced by motor buses, the scene was set for further deliveries of Routemasters to replace the RT family through the rest of the decade and well into the next. New models of buses promisingly exhibited at the annual Earl's Court Commercial Motor Show seem to have had little impact on the senior management and planning staff of London Transport. While much of the rest of Britain's bus operating industry was keen to embrace the developing rear-engined vehicle concept, particularly at first for double-deck buses, LT at the time appeared – to outsiders at least – to be continuing with the policy of 'stick with what you know works well'. Such conservatism paid dividends only in the eventual nostalgic romanticism of the front-engined, rear-loading double-deck bus at the time when London had been completely left behind by the rest of Britain.

Further Routemaster developments were thus proceeded with, simultaneously paying only lip service at first to what to many was the writing on the wall. The only true front entrance design to achieve a front position for the engine as well was the Guy Wulfrunian, a somewhat unfortunate model of no interest to LT.

The historical arrangement whereby AEC was to supply the lion's share of chassis and mechanical components remained in place at the start of the decade, allowing LT to follow its chosen option of dual sourcing. This was achieved during the RT build period by contracting Leyland Motors to manufacture somewhat more than one third of the type requirement. Rather than divide Routemaster mechanics into unworkable small quantities, the two sub frames' manufacture was kept with AEC; Leyland received the contract to build a sizeable minority of the engines. Then, Leyland merged with Associated Commercial Vehicles. The point of the equitable sharing of manufacturing was thereby lost.

The next item in 1962's double-deck story is the introduction of the Routemaster coach, intended to replace the ubiquitous RF on many existing Green Line routes and the east London RT-worked routes. It was not seen as the instrument to remodel the routes themselves, merely as a means of reducing the service frequency. RMC 4 had been one of the first four trial Routemasters (and the only one to be bodied by the state-owned Eastern Coach Works at Lowestoft) and had shown itself to be a popular vehicle with passengers and operating crew. Sixty-eight RMCs were ordered to the basic bus design but with an improved ride quality by employing air suspension at the rear. Greater comfort was provided in several ways, not least in the back platform being fully enclosed, a considerable benefit in keeping out road dirt on higher speed journeys. The seating capacity was lowered to 57 in the interests of providing greater leg room. The seats themselves were deeper in the manner of the RF coaches, and had higher back rests – an improvement over the RFs. Parcels racks were located overhead, again following the RF example, and unlike the east London RTs that had none of these extra touches. The RMCs were equipped with the standard AEC AV590 engine, though Leyland engines were fitted to the standard buses numbered on either side of the coaches. Early in 1962 it had been expected for the RMCs to come into stock in the late summer, and that there would follow one year's operating experience before deciding whether to replace all the Green Line RFs with RMCs except on those routes obstructed by low bridges. In the event, the RMCs were welcomed earlier, starting in earnest in mid-July 1962.

A subject arising at the end of the replacement of trolleybuses in the summer of 1962 was a review of the life expectancy of the RT family in the light of their mechanical performance and overhaul systems. Aldenham Works was the central establishment responsible for handling the RT family in this regard to a pre-determined interval. The buses emerged from the works as virtually new ones, so long as certain parent garages, still responsible for manageable items such as engines and lesser mechanical parts, maintained or surpassed laid-down standards. So good was the quality of Aldenham's output that the interval between overhauls was extended more than once – and this when the buses were growing older and therefore it might have been expected that the interval would be shortened. Plans were amended in this 1962 review to allow withdrawal of the Leylands first, the last RTLs undergoing a fourth overhaul then withdrawal in the mid 1970s after the last RTWs in the early 1970s. Some RTs would be withdrawn before a sixth overhaul became due as late as 1977 – by this time it is likely that all would have been confined to the country area if all had gone to plan.

Ensuing from enhanced mechanical efficiency, a reduced engineering capability was needed, thereby setting in store some difficulties when faced with a desire, much later, for a return to greater maintenance and engineering requirements to help solve problems with some of the rear-engined vehicles we'll come to. One reason for taking the Leylands out of service before the AEC RTs was because they were less popular among drivers. One earlier short lived use was found for a mere 18 RTLs when they were repainted Lincoln green and despatched to Hatfield garage for use on the 303 pair of routes. Neither drivers nor engineering staff took to them, additional to which was the need to equip this single country department garage with Leyland spare parts. After slightly less than a year, at mid-summer 1961, the green Leylands were replaced by the better liked RTs, and then began to take over from the 1939-40 first RTs on driver training work from central area garages.

Noticeable was the absence of the shorter length Routemaster buses in future plans for the country department. A single somewhat cheaper double decker was provided by AEC from its new range which re-introduced the model name 'Renown'. RX 1, as it came to be called unofficially, worked from Northfleet garage to see how well it stood the fairly arduous route 480. No orders followed; instead, RMLs came to work the route and some others in the country area beginning in autumn 1965.

Fifty red liveried Atlanteans came in the second half of 1965 to be compared in service with a two-person crew alongside RMLs from four north London central area garages, though not at the same time. In build at Park Royal Coachworks at the same time were the eight Lincoln green liveried Fleetlines destined for trial from East Grinstead garage. Though intended to be worked with conductors at peak times and as one-man operation outside the peaks (with the upper deck barred out of use), it is believed they were never worked in this latter method, always carrying a conductor at this time. In the next year the eight Fleetlines were exchanged with a like number of central area Atlanteans for direct comparison. The outcome could well have had an effect on the later decision to opt wholeheartedly for the Fleetline, a handful of which were ordered at the very end of the decade, to become the precursors of the DMS age. Afterwards the Fleetlines returned to their former country haunts and now were worked in a dual fashion as first intended.

The possibility of adapting the basic Routemaster principle to produce a rear engined version – still employing a two-person crew – had not been overlooked, and to this end, several sets of parts were gathered, one of which materialised as FRM 1 in 1966. Its first revenue earning work did not follow until June 1967 when it joined the Atlanteans at Tottenham garage. Once repaired after an unfortunate fire incident, the bus (now with some openable windows) came back to Tottenham. By the decade's end, the bus had been adapted for one-man working and was sent to work on the quieter, if uninspiring, route linking the Roundshaw Estate (built on a part of London's original southern commercial airport) at Croydon with the town centre, hidden away as though an embarrassment to LT who now realised it was far too late to develop the FRM as first conceived.

A more successful variant on the Routemaster theme was also developed in the mid-1960s: the natural successor to the RMC Green Line coach was to utilise the RML's overall length and construct a body in the same style as the RMC to produce the RCL. Several tinkerings with the frontal design produced a more cohesive appearance and, to those who rode on them, the RCLs gave what was generally agreed the most comfortable ride of any of the variants. In the same way as the earlier RMCs, they had independent suspension at the front, air suspension at the rear and a heating system made efficient by the rear platform being fully enclosed. The improved ride quality came from the longer wheelbase; front tyres were of a slightly sturdier specification. Introduced on route 721 out of Aldgate in June 1965, they brought a deserved touch of luxury, as much an improvement over the RTs they replaced on the east London routes as the RTs themselves had been over their early post-war Daimler predecessors.

Through the mid-1960s, with so many Routemasters coming on stream, large quantities of RTs and RTLs were sold, many to overseas customers whose rule of the road, to drive on the left, suited the surplus London vehicles that were shipped to Ceylon (Sri Lanka) and South Africa. Many RTWs were also despatched to Ceylon, while others were distributed in penny lots around central area garages for use as driver trainers. London evening newspapers carried a small advertisement in their Situations Vacant columns at the time aiming to recruit new driving staff by offering a free trial drive of a London bus from the applicant's local garage. Those who accepted the offer found themselves, after gentle interrogation as to their driving experience, at the wheel of an RTW for a 30-minute drive through local suburbia, an introductory experience never to be forgotten.

The Transport (London) Bill gained royal assent in 1969 to become the Act under which the central area was to report to the Greater London Council from 1st January 1970 instead of to the Minister of Transport, while the Country Bus & Coach Department would remain under state ownership as a member company of the National Bus Company, set up under the previous year's Transport Act. This major change was to herald a sharp contrast in vehicle policies between the red and green bus operators.

PRIVATE
"BLACK & WHITE"
SCOTCH WHISKY
FXT 270

Visible body sag along the lower deck windows of RT 95 (*left*) betrays its timber framing to the bodywork, constructed in spring 1940 at London Transport's own Chiswick bus works past which sister RT 114 (*right*) will be driven in a few minutes' time after having negotiated Gunnersbury roundabout before the M4 flyover was built. Many operators use buses and coaches no longer in good enough condition for front line passenger use to train novice drivers; London Transport would often remove most seats so that a reduced vehicle excise duty could be paid. Red RT 95, caught in early 1960s' period traffic of Scammell articulated lorry and Walls' sausages delivery van at Ravenscourt Park, has its front roof route number box panelled over. Both buses were disposed of in 1963, RT 114 being considered unworthy of preservation and so passing through a West London dealer to an Attleborough (Norfolk) concern that removed the tired bodywork and passed the chassis for possible spare parts to an operator near Norwich. *Both Tony Belton*

Taking a rest in warm August sunshine in 1960 are three driving trainer buses – green RT 36 and next to it, RTs 110 and 118. The green RT had been one of seven of the first production type to gain a country area livery especially to work out of Hertford garage on route 327 which crossed a weight-limited bridge over the New River. After the bridge had been rebuilt, allowing the slightly heavier post-war RTs to use it, RT 36 joined many of its red peers on 'learner' duties. Both red RTs show an 'L' plate in the nearside front window, well shaded by the canopy above, on Barking garage's hard standing. *David Stevens*

By the early 1960s, the oldest bodywork incorporating London's historic route number display housed in its dedicated roofbox and coded as the RT3 type was being dispersed randomly throughout the range of fleet numbers after overhaul. Park Royal Vehicles and Weymann's of Addlestone were selected as the outside manufacturers when LT realised it would be in no position to build all its requirements itself. The two firms produced virtually identical bodywork. RT 1314 (*above*) at Edgware Underground station shows the early arrangement of vertical route number display on the nearside front corner pillar, thankfully superseded by a more readable illuminated number above it under the canopy. RT 3956 (*below*) pauses outside a factory in rain-drenched Edgware Road, Colindale, en route for Stanmore Underground station, a more reasonable destination for route 245 when replacing the previous trolleybus 645 that turned short at Canons Park. The whole design hangs together in workmanlike practicality whose in-service experience lessons were learnt during wartime service on forerunners RT 1 and RT 2-151. *Both: Tony Belton*

In 1963 and before the advent of bus lanes, Piccadilly became a one-way street eastbound at the eastern end. Pall Mall and St James's Street came to be used in the westbound route diversion for Piccadilly and RT 2686 demonstrates such use as it passes over a pedestrian crossing whose refuge sign still proclaims NO ENTRY in words. The deep nearside valence below the canopy was carried over from the original RT design. It was absent from later buses – as shown on the next page. It had been a curious hangover from the 1930s. Leyland bodywork fitted to its Titan TD4 chassis in 1936 had omitted the valence to produce a cleaner line. *Howard Butler*

On the Barnet road near North Finchley in October 1961 we see Saunders bodied RT 4231, a stock number allocated to this bodybuilder's second batch of fifty RTs when built. No reason has ever come forward for the positioning of the offside route number further back, but it was a not unattractive feature of these vehicles. Perhaps Saunders just wanted to make its mark on a body that in all other respects was indistinguishable from the Park Royal and Weymann RT10s, such was the accuracy with which the bodybuilder followed LT's drawings. *Ian Stewart*

It had always been rare for an independent operator to run a service within the central bus area, but in the years after the turning point of the 1958 busmen's strike, several were begun, even using former LT vehicles. In 1963, at Gidea Park station, the one time RT 207 now looks smart in Upminster & District's livery, to which operator the bus had been sold in the recent February. A 'lazy' blind clearly based on LT's style gives details of the route, without distraction from commercial advertising, unlike Saunders-bodied RT 1797 opposite which shows a range of attractions for the motoring competition at the rear. The illuminated stop light above RT 1797's registration number plate is showing amber, the correct hue at the time. *Fred Ivey*

A first model Vauxhall Victor accelerates away from the police traffic light in June 1962 followed by three RTs while RT 4281 passes down-at-heel shops and flats opposite in Ilford High Road. In passing a redundant trolleybus overhead support pole, RT 3843 heads towards the photographer to continue its 145 journey to the once well known Royal Forest Hotel at Chingford, located on the western edge of Epping Forest. *David Stephens*

Catford garage's RT 1219 with the later 'roofbox' bodywork of the RT10 type stands comparison with the RT3 low-valence variety pulling in behind on route 78 to stand at the Shoreditch Church terminus. On the RT10 body, the earlier RT3 corner pillar vertical route number display was replaced by a horizontal number display under the canopy. The released pillar position was now used to secure the vertical box housing a semaphore trafficator, though this was not in use by the time of this photo. *Fred Ivey*

London Transport's traditional displays of route points could be of great help in confirming an unfamiliar passenger's need – except when they were wrongly displayed as here on RT 3554 with RT10 body; the via points shown are for the 138! At this time and for many years after, London buses continued to be equipped with a low level nearside front fog lamp, generally held to be of some help to the driver in picking his way through dense fog in the days before near-universal smokeless zones. *Capital Transport*

As dusk draws near, Catford Town Hall in 1961 has five members of the RT family in view. Catford garage's RT 3390 showing route 124 blinds stands in front of a part obscured RTL with sidelights illuminated on the Blackwall Tunnel route 108 to Crystal Palace and RT 3963 on the fairly short lived tram replacement number, 179. With two typical RT types passing about their business along Rushey Green in the background, the planned principle of standardisation is seen to be achieved. *Capital Transport*

It must be Sunday! Barking garage continued to run RTs on route 9 on this day when the Monday-Saturday service had been modernised in 1963 by Routemasters from Dalston and Mortlake garages. Unwashed RT 3041 circumnavigates Hyde Park Corner chasing even dirtier RT 3784. Both have their lower radiators blanked off though RT 3041 has an extra, unofficial, sheet above the black version. The under-canopy route number, now on a blind able to be lit from behind, could be seen as an improvement over the earlier vertical attempt.

In 1966, Uxbridge garage was still located just inside the country area, along Oxford Road in Denham, Bucks, at the time its RT 4528 was photographed awaiting another train replacement journey from Baker's Road which serves as Uxbridge's bus station and as an approach to the Underground station. The two RTs scheduled for working the 225 carried few passengers. Much of the former Western Region branch line trackbed to Staines West station through Poyle and Yeoveney was later obliterated by the M25 motorway. A Garston garage RML stands with its back to the camera, waiting to depart on route 347 through Harefield by circling the island outside the station entrance and driving past the empty RT. *Capital Transport*

Holloway garage's RT 2045 leads the largely unpainted RM 664 (Highgate garage) southwards along Whitehall in August 1961. Though both buses look smart, the 'silver' appearance of the trial Routemaster became dull within months. A comparison may be drawn here between the two sets of front route information: the RT with the route number to the nearside, RM on offside; and the Routemaster's smaller route aperture allowing mention of three place names against the RT's four lines (and six place names) though in the same size of lettering. In later years, such standards of information presentation were to be envied by many. *Bruce Jenkins*

An immaculate RT 4651 heads along Rye Lane, Peckham in 1968, past the 1932 built Co-Operative store towards the southern extremity of the long 12 route at South Croydon – whose garage was not home to this bus, which instead was well looked after at Elmers End, a garage rebuilt after destruction by an enemy V1 flying bomb in July 1944. 'Flake' grey has made an appearance as the midway relief colour, replacing cream. The use of a side/rear aperture route blind in the front provided a third confirmation of the route number on approach. The offside route number plate practice has long since ceased, though its holder can still be made out behind the rearmost lower deck window. *Capital Transport*

FREMLINS
'ELEPHANT' BEERS
VIA TOWN CENTRE
801
PIN GREEN
RT 1362
KXW 481

BRANDY make sure it's MARTELL
KENTISH TIMES YOUR BEST LOCAL
SINGLEWELL ROAD
WROTHAM ROAD
NEW ROAD
STONEBRIDGE ROAD
487
GYPSY CORNER
KYY 538

Above left The last vestiges of snowfall outside the Lloyds branch bank at Stevenage bus station in January 1966 point to the cause of the dirty condition of these two RTs loaned to the country area, some of a number sent to the local garage at this time because of its own RTs being put out of action by the freezing conditions. Earlier in the decade, some red RTs had replaced green 'roofbox' RTs for withdrawal and disposal. RT 1382 has Stevenage garage's code painted on to prefix the running number, while sister behind may have been a more short term transfer as it employs an alloy stencil garage plate. *Capital Transport*

Left A red RT going to Gypsy Corner in April 1966 could perhaps have been expected to be on route 187 passing through North Acton rather than on the country 487 showing this destination, a short working south of Gravesend. RT 1711 heading east along a barren London Road had been allocated to Northfleet garage long enough to have relevant front posters. *Barry Le Jeune*

Above A red bus loaned to the country area for a different reason: RT 3086 was one of a number drafted into Leatherhead garage to cover for its own green RTs that had had their electrics damaged by River Mole flood water in September 1966. Evidence of having been rushed into service is provided by the chalked route number displays as passengers are collected outside another Lloyds bank, this time at Leatherhead. *Capital Transport*

Working the longest route in the detached Essex Thames-side operation of the country area, RT 4043 heads along a rather uninspiring St Mary's Lane towards Upminster Bridge station while another disappears in the distance towards Tilbury. The mudguards and lifeguard rail of country buses were customarily painted in the main livery colour, unlike their central red cousins, which, apart from a short experiment in the early 1950s, were traditionally finished in black. *Howard Butler*

RT 651 was the ultimate member of the first batch of post-war RTs delivered country buses in 1948. All of them had Park Royal 'roofbox' bodies, and this one was allocated to Watford High Street garage. Here, it is taking a break at one of Guildford's bus stations. Co-incidentally, Guildford garage's RT 1026, behind, had the same history, having also originally carried a roofbox body when allocated to the same Watford garage. *Malcolm Young*

A fully laden RT 3139 from Leatherhead garage turns into the final furlong on special route 406F before evicting its passengers at Epsom Downs racecourse. The bookie (or would he prefer 'turf accountant'?) on the platform is clearly intent on being first away. Let's hope he jumps off left foot first otherwise he'll have a hard landing! The hoarding should leave no doubt where to pick up the homeward bus.
Alan Osborne

Although six green RTs can clearly be seen, a red RT family vehicle can also just be made out in the depths of Garston garage's running shed in March 1966, probably a training bus. With blue blinds yet to be set for its next departure, RT 3011 fronts the trio of RTs parked on the terminal access road, itself accommodating a fourth RT, seen sideways-on behind the office block to the left. Blue blinds had become established practice to indicate an express service – omitting many of the stops – a colour distinction likely to be lost on much of the travelling public. The bus stop flag indicates the boarding point for short working route 347 journeys leaving for the Uxbridge direction, a rare example of accepted public access within garage precincts beyond an office area. Garston garage was built to replace the two Watford garages of which Leavesden Road was closed in June 1952 upon Garston's opening. *Capital Transport*

Above right Windsor was still a popular destination for a summer's day out by public transport in 1966, witnessed here by the royal borough's garage forecourt as a hub of activity. From the left, a crew has a friendly exchange by the RF showing a blind for 704, Tunbridge Wells, while country bus RT 1526's driver awaits the arrival of his conductor before setting off as a relief back across London to Harlow. A cap-less conductor walks past the platform of another RT on Green Line relief duty, judging by the blank blind above him, as a group is engaged in hearing a driver's answers at an RC's doorway. Standards of staff uniform are various from white-topped cap to no head gear and from serge jacket to light grey summer coat. *Alan Osborne*

Right Green Line RT 3229, looking very presentable, heads eastward along Ilford High Road on the 721 for Brentwood in June 1962. The Bedford TK lorry behind – perhaps on a trunk journey too judging by the headboard – overtakes a local RT in the run up to the police controlled traffic lights. The RT numbered 3229 was later in red livery and is recorded as being sold to a Yorkshire scrap merchant in April 1975. *David Stevens*

GREEN LIN
RELIEF
718
HARLOW
DON'T BE VAGUE
Ask for
Haig
T.H.JENNINGS (HARLOW POOLS) LTD.
2/3 THE ROWS, 32 THE STOW, REGISTERED OFFICE 59/60 THE STOW
OPEN AN ACCOUNT TODAY WITH HARLOW'S LEADING FIRM
TURF AND FOOTBALL Accountants
RT 1526
HA
LONDON TRANSPORT
KGU 240

GREENWOODS TRAVEL GOODS
GIDEA PARK ROMFORD
GOODMAYES ILFORD
STRATFORD BOW
721
BRENTWOOD
BARTRUM'S
NORFOLK LONDON
713 HBJ
KYY 958
brahams
for distinctive furniture
brahams
DISTINCTIVE
FURNITURE
SOPASALE

The rush hour on a warm September morning in 1968 with pedestrians, three buses and a Thames Trader tipper lorry all trying to attain Turnpike Lane and its bus station, only a few yards ahead. RT 255 had some more life in it until its withdrawal from service less than two years later. All three buses would terminate at the Turnpike Lane Underground interchange, the Merlin bringing up the rear running on the new short distance 'satellite' route W1 from the North Circular crossroads at the Cambridge public house, Edmonton, exactly duplicating not only the 144 over this part of its time-honoured route, but also the 217 and 231. It could be seen to have precious little advantage in this case over the 144 as it descends the slope off the bridge across the one-time Palace Gates branch railway line. *Capital Transport*

Above right Much has changed around Ferndale Street – neighbouring the former Royal Albert Dock – since this June 1965 photograph was taken. RT 2776, still featuring the extra ventilators in the front roof dome after its continental drive across North America some 13 years previously, stood at this terminus, a short turn for route 101, but a peak hour extension for the 147 behind. The wind on this day may have been gusty enough to produce the vanishing windscreen wiper phenomenon: all three buses' wipers are fouling the cream band. Alternatively, Upton Park garage drivers may have purposely pushed the parked wipers beyond their line of vision. With its half-width doorway open, the timekeeping inspector's hut stands back to the handy Ferndale refreshment facility. *Capital Transport*

Right Equipped with a bright yellow-gold fleetname in this September 1967 picture, RT 1806 awaits departure from Edgware station forecourt. The bus with this fleet number some 16 years previously would have been among scores of those stored on nearby open-air standing at Edgware garage awaiting introduction into tram replacement work. A time check clock cabinet is available for confirming the crew's cards behind the bus. If the sprinter is running for the bus, he hasn't noticed there's no driver. *Capital Transport*

99
TEA
FROM THE CO-OP
MANOR PARK
HIGH STREET NORTH
EAST HAM MANOR WAY
ROYAL ALBERT DOCK
101
WANSTEAD STATION
PEARL assurance
Haig
in every
Home
FERNDALE
SNACK BAR
TEAS SNACKS
FERNDALE STREET
LYR 827

Dunnsmanship
the art of
dressing better
for less
The Dirty Dozen
EASTCOTE LANE
HARROW ON THE HILL
WEALDSTONE
STANMORE CANONS PK
114
RUISLIP STATION
LONDON TRANSPORT
KYY 661
MARTINI

Typifying an early 1960s' period piece, a young mother pushes her pram past the primitive passenger shelter with no thought of boarding RT 3857 for the ride to Slough railway station and the walk to the town centre. Being long before the advent of low-floor buses, such baby carriage equipment was denied the chance of a ride. The weather is warm, judging by the open windows and lunchtime imbibers standing outside Charrington brewery's 'George' inn, the short route 446's northern terminus. *John Boylett*

Running only on Wednesdays and Sundays to coincide with the visiting times to the hospital shown as the destination on RT 2982, route 472 was seldom seen. Passengers were conveyed only from the points listed in the public timetable to the hospital, just off the Brighton Road east of Hooley. RT 2982 makes haste uphill early in a sunny December afternoon in 1966. *Alan Osborne*

Many serviceable postwar RT-family buses became surplus to needs from the mid 1950s and into the 1960s. Next to go after the 2RTs were the 120 Cravens-bodied examples, starting in April 1956. Former RT 1487 leaves the Chiswick factory of the Permutit water softening equipment firm in a plain but not unattractive two-tone blue paint scheme. Flashing trafficators have been added since LT ownership, at the front on the nearside corner pillar and at the back within what here is the white medial band. Only one other Cravens-bodied RT became an employer's staff bus, and apart from RT 1420 damaged in a low bridge accident, the remaining 117 all found new ownership with bus operators throughout England and Scotland. *Tony Belton*

The Buckinghamshire independent operator Red Rover Omnibus Ltd had had operational experience of the 2RT2 model and when the opportunity came to buy the postwar version in good condition, he took it with some enthusiasm. The leader of these two, caught in Aylesbury's traffic, is former RT 1668, fitted with an RT3 body and so a candidate for early withdrawal from LT service. The roofbox and LT's wheel furniture have been removed. *Barry Le Jeune*

East India Dock Road
Commercial Road
Aldgate London Bdg
Elephant Camberwell
40A
BLACKWALL TUNNEL
aig
in
every
OCAL
HOTEL
HOME
DON'T BE
VAGUE
Ask for
Haig
SCOTCH WHISK
40A
OLD 780

Left Apart from a dented nearside front wing, a perfectly presented RTL 1561 heads the line up of five Leylands inside Poplar garage, formerly Poplar trolleybus depot, in June 1966. The rear RTL on the right carries an RT10 roofbox type body. All appears clean and tidy, giving no clue to the decline in efficiency brought about partly by chronic staff shortage. *Capital Transport*

Above About to leave the shadowy confines of Victoria bus station, our driver has a word with someone on the narrow footway before engaging second gear and setting off for the home garage at Tottenham. This was the last night of the 7ft 6ins width Leyland RTs on route 76, to be replaced by Routemasters and XAs on the morrow. RTL 524 was not deleted from LT stock till February 1970 when it was just one of 33 similar buses consigned to a Barnsley scrapyard. *Tony Belton*

In the heyday of route 49 when it was still able to be reasonably punctual in running its long Crystal Palace – Shepherd's Bush journey, RTL 643 virtually unnoticeably crosses over the West London railway line with only the slightly rising pavement on both sides and double kerb opposite giving small clues. The newsvendor's stand cheerfully blocks much of the former station entrance. The Birmingham-built Metro-Cammell bodywork mounted on the 450 Leyland chassis RTL 551-1000 appeared outwardly to be virtually identical to the standard product of Park Royal and Weymann, the only noticeable difference being the generous beading above the cream relief, making the band appear shallower. However, so little wood was used in building the bodywork that the term 'all-metal' has been applied in describing it, a feature supported by an increased vehicle weight of 5cwt over the other two makers' products. A different method of securing the body to chassis meant that the bodies were not interchangeable with the standard model and with only one exception they were routinely kept within their dedicated batch upon overhaul at Aldenham works. They soon gained a reputation for sturdiness and freedom from rattles – features shared with RF type single deckers from the same bodybuilder. *Tony Belton*

Right Poplar garage's RTL 954 takes a break alongside a Romford RCL on the Minories bus and coach station's familiar fan-patterned stone setts before heading back east on another rush hour short working in August 1965. The mountings in the cream relief band for the front flashing trafficators were differently designed from those fitted to the Weymann and Park Royal bodies. The route blind is set in error for the Saturday/Sunday route 40. *Capital Transport*

Right Eighteen RTLs were repainted green for Country Department service and sent to Hatfield garage in July 1960. They were not popular with drivers, who for one thing would have found their steering heavier than on the AEC version. Another difference was the engine stop procedure. The Leyland required an upward pull on a stirrup alongside the steering column – easier to reach by hand than the accelerator pedal of the AEC, which needed a sharp and sustained reverse pull to achieve a stopped engine, accomplished for many by an upward flick of the driver's foot from behind the pedal. After only roundly a year's service from Hatfield, the buses returned to the central area, for use in driver training. *Ian Stewart*

Did the neighbours mind? Battersea garage's Metro-Cammell-bodied RTL 968 heads the line of parked up buses during the August 1964 Epsom races. A revealing statistic from 1960 was that for the Derby in June that year, the first time the race was televised, the Morden service carried 27 per cent fewer passengers than it did for the previous Derby. Despite this drop, these otherwise quiet residential streets near Tattenham Corner station played host to the 35 buses laying over before returning punters on the lengthy seven-mile express service back to Morden Underground station at the end of the day's racing. Traditionally a central buses' operation, double deckers of greater age would be drawn from across the network to support the race-day only operation, though by now virtually all the buses would be from the RT family. Despite warm weather, the resting driver sits in his cab smartly attired in collar and tie and cap topped by the summertime white crownpiece. *John Boylett*

THIS TUNNEL CONSTRUCTED BY THE LONDON COUNTY COUNCIL
PRINCE OF WALES K.G.
OF JUNE 1908
82
Rotherhithe Tunnel
Lower Road
Redriff Road
Rotherhithe Street
ROTHERHITHE BRUNEL ROAD
Nevada Smith
PLAZA
Nevada Smith
PLAZA
NLE 712

Opposite With sidelights and saloon lights switched on, RT10-bodied RTL 1438 emerges from the comparative gloom of the less well known Rotherhithe tunnel beneath the Thames, which according to the proclamation above, had been opened by the future King George V some 58 years before this September 1966 picture. The narrow carriageway is evident, needing special care by the driver to avoid chafing the tyres against the kerb. *Capital Transport*

The nominally older Metro-Cammell-bodied RTL 761 heads away from the photographer bound for central London and Southfields on route 39, while approaching is a younger RTL 1096, sold off in March 1964 to the Bishop's Stortford coach operator, some time before this stretch of Seven Sisters Road near the Nag's Head was made one-way northound in January 1965. Despite some livery changes, the LT radiator badge remains. *Tony Belton*

KENT
K
MESSENGER
HAMMERSMITH
FULHAM BROADWAY
CHELSEA VICTORIA
CHARING CROSS BANK
11
KENT
M
MESSENGER
LIVERPOOL ST
FINSBURY CIRCUS
Famous for flavour
NELSON
LONDON TRANSPORT
RTW 127
KGK 627

Left Lugging the fully laden RTW 127 from Hammersmith's Butterwick bus station through route 11's dense traffic must have been tiring for the uniformed driver on a warm May day in 1965. Dalston's work-spattered wide Leyland has run out as the first duty of the day on the 11, and still uses a route blind of the style which began to be replaced after November 1961 by blinds with lower case lettering, believed to be easier to read. Despite not being taut in the frame, the blind here is eminently readable, employing suitably letterspaced Johnston capitals. *Barry Le Jeune*

Above Flashing trafficators had been tried first in 1956. Three years later they began to be fitted retrospectively to all motor buses. RTW 91 clearly demonstrates the equipment in this 1961 photograph of a busy Catford scene. Trials using the wide Leyland had been conducted in 1950 to see whether their extra width made difficulties for them to be driven through innermost London. It did not, so paving the way for the type to be used on cross-city routes such as the 176 and, later, universal Routemaster availability. *Capital Transport*

The yard in front of Lillie Bridge Underground depot is where these two RTWs are resting in between trips on the 74 one day in October 1960. Both allocated to Putney garage, RTW 304 has yet to receive the trafficator arms already fitted to 313, a fitment programme in progress in the late 1950s and early 1960s. London Transport itself uses the front poster positions on both RTWs, the first for staff and the second for commercial advertising. *Ian Stewart*

Facing page Clad with advertisements for both Battersea funfair and the Festival Gardens some eleven years after their 1951 opening to celebrate the Festival of Britain, RTW 279 waits in Camden Town for another journey to the more salubrious Chelsea, leaving a sister bus to follow soon, while RTW 284 circles the block to take a deserved break, carefully avoiding a parked Heinkel bubblecar. The widely spaced rear advertisements are so placed as to clear the small rubber buffers, just discernible, on which the upper deck emergency exit window was meant to rest if opened. Were that residential streets were so free from parked cars nowadays. *Tony Belton*

BATTERSEA FUN FAIR
OPEN DAILY
SWISS COTTAGE
KILBURN
NOTTING HILL GATE
KENSINGTON
31
CHELSEA
Get on the trail of the happiest ale
BEN TRUMAN
BAYHAM STREET NW1
GREENLAND ROAD
NO ENTRY
LONDON TRANSPORT
KXW 379

31
SWISS COTTAGE KILBURN
NOTTING HILL GATE
KENSINGTON
CAMDEN TOWN
Cook with ketchup
Heinz of course
WATCH YOUR STEP
VIC 8484 - 1962 MODELS
GODFREY DAVIS
SELF DRIVE · CHAUFFEUR DRIVEN
KXW 384

Not for the only time Victoria Street has been closed, entailing a diversion for the many routes that used it in the mid-1960s. RTW 243 starts away from the Great Peter Street crossing as the traffic lights change, with RM 1754 and another close behind in Great Smith Street – all could catch up with the trio *below* where Great Smith has become Marsham Street hosting RTW 239, another wide Leyland and finally an RT10 type on the 134 to Pimlico as they line up to cross Horseferry Road traffic lights. Westminster Council was evidently a late convert to modern electric street lighting in view of the elegant, but outdated, gas lights, one sandwiched between the traffic signals at Great Peter Street corner, another just emerging from behind RTW 239. The British Legion car park (3 shillings, 15p, daily!) has long since gone, but the organisation continues to provide parking wardens. *Both: Howard Butler*

Although route 1 had seen the final change to RTW operation – though only on Saturdays – in January 1965 from Willesden garage, the ultimate route on which the type was operated was the 95. RTW 494 passes its home garage; RMs released from Putney garage by the arrival of new RMLs would replace Brixton's RTWs in May 1966, within a week or so of this picture being taken. *Capital Transport*

London Transport once had a policy of employing double deck buses wherever practically possible, even where low railway bridges or Thames tunnels may have suggested otherwise. A case in point was the Headstone Drive London Midland main line bridge at Wealdstone, necessitating a special design of double decker to pass beneath. The RLH was based on AEC's standard postwar Regent chassis, as opposed to London's special 0961 version for the RT, fitted with bodywork built with reduced headroom by Weymann at Addlestone (Surrey) to a design used for buses in the provinces. This less than ideal 'lowbridge' arrangement was kept to the absolute minimum, with a mere 76 buses in the class forming only just over one per cent of the double deck fleet. RLH 59 was one of the second batch of 56 dating from 1952. In March 1968 the bus passes beneath the offending bridge whose carriageway had been widened some years previously, when no opportunity was taken to lower it. As it was, it was liable to flooding at times of heavy rain. The bus was withdrawn in the next year. *Capital Transport*

The RLH type was allocated in small batches around much of the LT area, central and country. Representative of the far eastern contingent in central buses is RLH 69 at Hall Lane, Cranham on the very short 248 route before its natural westward extension past its Hornchurch home garage to Romford. Generally conductors disliked working this lowbridge type with its very restricted headroom on the upper deck, whose seat backs can be seen at high level through the windows. With a sunken gangway on the offside and single wide seats for four passengers each, collecting fares from passengers seated against the nearside meant stretching across the front of up to three others. In a fully laden bus it was quite usual for intermediate passengers to assist conducting by passing fare money, tickets and change to and fro, encouraging friendly exchanges and a pleasant atmosphere – till they rose to alight, and perhaps forgot to bend thereby hitting their head on the low ceiling. Despite the provincial-style Weymann bodywork seating three fewer passengers than the 56-seat RT, conducting an RLH on a short busy journey was no enviable task. *Gerald Mead*

Both RLH 32 and RF 644 look to be in smart order here at the Duke's Head, Brighton Road stop at Addlestone in May 1967. The area south west from London was – occasionally still is – bedevilled by inadequate railway bridges built in Victorian times for horse-drawn traffic of the period by the London & South Western Railway, often needing lowbridge buses to comply with LT's ambition of operating double deckers wherever possible. Addlestone garage, 250 yards to the right along Station Road behind the buses, provided this bus, though Guildford garage was allocated RLHs as well. The last London Country RLHs were withdrawn from these two garages in August 1970. The rustic area behind the fence, and including the public house, has since been replaced by local council buildings. *Barry Le Jeune*

In December 1966, Dalston garage's RLH 54 portrays inner east London's only lowbridge bus route, with evidence of World War II enemy action and subsequent partial repair as a backdrop (*above*) while (*below*) the first bus of the second batch, RLH 21, performs an equally short journey through Guildford's suburban village of Merrow in May 1968. The route traversed no low height obstacles, so had no need of an RLH. Indeed, at this point in the journey, from the paucity of passengers, a minibus would have sufficed. *Both: Alan Osborne*

Green RLH 27 turns from Imperial Drive into its terminus at Rayners Lane while on loan to Harrow Weald garage some time after May 1967, the month in which the new Green Line route 727 started. The conductor, suitably attired for a warm day in open neck shirt, rolled sleeves and sunglasses, avoids internal claustrophobia by riding on the open platform. *Colin Brown*

The only double decker to be bodied by Eastern Coach Works for London Transport was one of the four prototypes, CRL 4, reclassified to RMC 4 in August 1961. The Leyland-engined coach stands opposite the entrance to Epping garage on 27th April 1963. Livery has reverted to Lincoln green after a spell in the experimental lighter shade until the previous November, and appears to be admired by two gentlemen at the combined bus/coach stop. It was the only Routemaster coach to have the bus-style three-piece front destination display. *Tony Wild*

Trolleybus route 607 had become the 207 when Routemasters from Hanwell took over on 9th November 1960, but for 18 months there were still trolleybuses at Shepherd's Bush. K1 class 1116 comes in towards an errant pedestrian and the photographer on the south-east side of the Green: the electric buses finally ran on the 657 out of Isleworth depot on 8th May 1962, the end of London's trolleybus operations. RM 525's blind has already been wound to show its departing destination, having come along the Uxbridge Road.
Tony Belton

Only on a Sunday, and then only for six months in 1961, could Routemasters be seen working on the highest numbered red bus route, like RM 585 taking a break here at Finsbury Square, Moorgate. It was the sole example in the trolleybus replacement scheme of the diesel and electrically-powered vehicles running together on the same route, hence the Highgate-garaged RM displaying the trolleybus destination. Route 609 became the 104 upon full Routemaster succession. The bus shows its as-built appearance, before detail changes were made in later years, many of them at the front. *Tony Belton*

Routemasters continued the practice of building the two decks separately, only coming together at a stage later than that shown here inside the Park Royal Vehicles works in 1960. Four RMs are well under construction, with their lower decks to the left of the uppers, all facing forward away from the photographer, who took his picture at the end of a shift judging by the absence of personnel and low level lighting. Later health and safety standards would involve a rather different approach to the workplace. *Bruce Jenkins*

Perhaps someone had by now realised that in very cold temperatures, the Routemaster's cooling system was prone to freezing up. The leader of these four RMs clearly expects the cold snap to continue, evidenced by the white sheet obscuring much of its radiator. RM 85, allocated to West Ham at the time of this January 1962 picture, shows the fixed window panes at the upper deck front as fitted to the production Routemasters to RM 253. The thin red strips at the window tops were scoops to direct air through ventilators set into the front dome to reduce summertime warmth for front passengers. They were found unsatisfactory. Opening front windows equipped all later built Routemasters. A lone trolleybus can just be made out between the tree trunks, due to head past the stopped buses here near the North Circular Road at Finchley. *Capital Transport collection*

Upon overhaul at Aldenham works, fresh advertisements were applied, and RM 11's show that the bus crew shortage is being addressed in one way, and that a box of matches cost 2½d (1p). The Poplar bus stands at the Canning Town short working stand before heading back to Chingford Mount on the trolleybus replacement route from North Woolwich, and typifies the appearance of the first production batch in the spring of 1963 before the many detailed changes that were made in later times. *R.C. Riley*

It's early in 1963 and the trees are not yet in leaf behind the London Co-operative Society's outpost of its shop in Epping High Street where RMC 1484 has pulled in to exchange crews opposite the bus garage, destined shortly to be closed. Heading for Aldgate on the 720A, the coach shows the short lived use of the offside route number blind in the panel enclosing the staircase on RMCs 1453–1520. *David Stevens*

Turning right from the short northern stretch of Regent Street into Oxford Street at Oxford Circus, RMC 1457 had been one of twelve Routemaster coaches sent new to Hertford garage to work Green Line route 715 jointly with eight out of Guildford starting in August 1962; purchase of RM coaches to replace the RFs on some routes had been approved more than two years earlier. Caught in a shaft of that December's morning sunlight, the coach carries plates for its partner garage on the lengthy route, and shows well its neat and functional appearance, though the black wording for the place names on amber-coloured background was not easy to read on the route blind. *Bruce Jenkins*

Resulting from the perceived success of leaving some aluminium panelled Underground carriages with a largely unpainted exterior, it was thought prudent to try the same thing on a bus – after all, it had been done elsewhere, notably in Liverpool, but had never become widespread in the United Kingdom. Economy was the fashionable catchword. Avoiding painting would not only reduce the cost of labour, time, materials, planning, supervision and accountancy, but there would be slightly less weight for the engine to propel around, thereby producing a tiny theoretical fuel cost saving too. RM 664 was the guinea pig. This bus happened to be the one quite by chance – no reason has been found for its particular selection. Non-aluminium parts were painted, in an aluminium-finish coating, such as the lifeguard rails, mudguards and bonnet, to match the main body. The 'unpainted' Routemaster entered service on 17th July 1961. The front view at Shepherd's Bush projects a rather unfinished appearance unattractively revealing many screw or rivet heads. The back of the bus showing the advertising dedication to a popular daily newspaper, was photographed leaving the Grove Park terminus of route 36B on a short working to Victoria in 1963, when working out of Rye Lane garage, Peckham. *Colin Brown, Howard Butler*

Well before London Bridge station bus forecourt was revamped, two city men walk along the roadway past a line of terminating Routemasters, the first two indicating short journeys on route 7. Leading RM 1760 will be going to its home garage known then as Middle Row in North Kensington, though labelled as Ladbroke Grove, the thoroughfare giving its name to the locality. When the garage was closed in 1981, its code X was handed on to the replacement Westbourne Park. RM 1765 behind won't reach the full weekday April 1966 destination of Acton's former tram depot, turning short at the Goldsmith's Arms, East Acton, and thereby perpetuating a long-standing custom brought over from horse bus days when it had been advantageous to water and rest horses at an accommodating hostelry. Both Routemasters now have the later style radiator grille with brightwork central strip and LT-style triangular badge, and both have lost their offside route number blind display at the staircase side, having been panelled across. *Capital Transport*

By June 1968 – witness the headlines on Victoria Underground station's street news-stand – Routemasters had long-since usurped RTWs on route 52. Victoria garage's RM 2053, like sister behind, retains the full depth intake below the front destination display but has lost its brake cooling grilles. The sidelong between decks site illuminates an advertisement for a brand of Scotch whisky, and is eminently readable from a distance unlike the cinema names on the front film-now-showing posters. *Colin Brown*

Complying with the policy that Routemasters provided with illuminated sidelong advertisements should be employed on those routes serving inner London, RM 2096's message implies that the effort is rather wasted. Oxford Street is as ever crowded with shoppers far more intent on their business than noticing this tidy bus heading for its route 137 northern terminus, let alone its posters, illuminated or not. *Capital Transport*

Above right The driver of RM 1905 has chosen to open the outer ventilation flap in the dash panel – often the more popular one of the two – but has left his sliding door open too on this warm day in August 1969. He'll change the flashing trafficator to the left as the bus leaves Morden Hall roundabout – the long brick wall encloses the park – for Morden's Northern Line terminus and bus station. *Capital Transport*

Right Perhaps due to the ever expanding Heathrow Airport and its perceived glamorous image, route 81B had seen an early change from RT to Routemaster operation in 1963. However, for connecting passengers off the Piccadilly tube at Hounslow East station before the tube's airport extension, there was the unwelcome hike along Kingsley Road to catch the bus here at the bus station on the south western flank of Hounslow's rebuilt bus garage. RM 1710 has lost the unnecessary brake cooling grilles at the base of the front wings and has its registration plate suspended beneath the engine grille rather than framed within its base line, a less fussy arrangement but leaving the plate susceptible to damage. The 1968 posters on the front portray the Round London Sightseeing Tour at a fare of six shillings (30p). *R. C. Riley*

TYRANT KING
93
Putney Wimbledon
South Wimbledon
Morden Nth Cheam
NORTH CHEAM
TYRANT KING
ALD 905B

98
223
PEARL
81B
Harlington Cnr
Cranford
Hounslow West Stn
HEATHROW AIRPORT CENTRAL
ROUND LONDON SIGHTSEEING TOUR
PAN AM
The shape of things to come: 747
81B
LONDON TRANSPORT
710 DYE

THE TYRANT KING
A LONDON ADVENTURE FOR CHILDREN
127
EDMONTON
TOTTENHAM
CAMDEN TOWN
WALTHAM CROSS
Face the future with PEARL assurance
CARLTON HOUSE
WLT 494

BOAC AIR TERMINAL
Silexine Paints welcomes you to London
11
HAMMERSMITH BDY
737 DYE

So comfortable was the ride given by the longer Routemaster coach that the passengers from east London would enjoy theirs to Whipsnade very much more than around 15 years earlier when relaxed wartime specification Daimlers had been the conveyances. Romford's RCL's had been introduced on route 726 in July 1965 and here, 2225 and 2228, twice the route's normal coach allocation, take a lengthy rest while their passengers tire themselves walking around the hilly acres of London's country zoo on that year's August Bank Holiday. *John Boylett*

Above left Route 127 had been trolleybus route 627 from Tottenham Court Road here to Waltham Cross, but when first changed to motor buses it was extended to Wilton Road at Victoria. RM 494 has turned short and waits in a side street off Tottenham Court Road for its next northbound journey. The bus retains hybrid frontal arrangements of blanked brake cooling grilles but with red vertical strip in engine grille and framed number plate. Its middle relief band has gone under a coat of all-consuming red paint. *John Herting*

Left The honour – or dishonour, whichever way it's looked upon – fell to RM 1737 to be the first all-over advertisement bus. In 1969 it was 'decorated' in this scheme, no doubt providing a welcome boost to the receipts in London Transport's advertising account. The bus collects passengers from the stop in Buckingham Palace Road close to Victoria Coach Station and outside the terminal building for British Overseas Airways Corporation. Did the bus wait for the trilby hatted gentleman? *Alan Osborne*

Delivered new in February 1966, RML 2398 here two months later at Becontree Heath bus stand, displays the smartest appearance achieved by the type. Poplar garage's bus is fully dressed for the Saturday route 5C service to cheer up the East End streets as it heads for a destination perhaps with more operational convenience than passenger needs. What price now for the blue police telephone box?
Barry Le Jeune

The country area RMLs stayed with the single headlamp concept in line with their red counterparts, and did not follow their Green Line RMC and RCL cousins in having twin lamps – though what need for them there was would have equalled the coaches' as the buses followed unlit country roads to much the same extent. Garston garage's RML 2440 month-old paintwork glistens in April 1966 sunshine as it collects a few more passengers for Uxbridge in an otherwise deserted Northwood, an area developed residentially in the 1920s and early 1930s by the erstwhile Metropolitan Railway through its Country Estates offshoot as 'Metroland'. *Barry Le Jeune*

A few minor modifications had been made to RMC 1469 in the late spring of 1964 as a prototype for the forthcoming RCLs. However, by the time of this February 1969 picture, a further overhaul had been undertaken and the modified body then took stock number RMC 1502, with RMC 1469 reverting to original format with a normal body – except that some features tried (and adopted) for the RCLs were then retrospectively introduced. Noteworthy here are the reduced depth saloon ventilator/heating grille to permit an unbroken relief colour line, no relief framing the windows, and changed fleetname styles and positions with no raised bullseye. A healthy passenger load awaits departure from St Mary's Square at Hitchin, then used as the town's bus station, in later years given over to the competition as a car park. Quite unusually, a London bus collects passengers while standing at right angles to the pavement with customary bus stop behind – an arrangement more comfortable perhaps for the Smiths coach alongside, on their stage service to Buntingford. *John Boylett*

The sidelong illuminated advertisement says it all – perhaps not quite all. It was known that some of the country department management held the opinion that Routemasters would be rather too refined – and expensive – for country bus work. Though this AEC-owned demonstration bus arrived at Aldenham works in August 1962, it wasn't until the next February that it started work out of Northfleet garage on the frequent route 480, Denton (Gravesend) – Dartford – Erith, alongside RTs. It's recorded as a 69 seater with forward entrance enclosed by jack-knife doors, and the regular AV 590 9.6 litre engine as fitted to bus Routemasters, but with AEC's Monocontrol drive. Though fitted up to carry garage and running number stencils, the bus was never labelled RX 1, its unofficial reference, and never carried LT fleetnames since it remained AEC's property. Here it rests outside the old Dartford garage in company with RF 217 in June 1963. No London Transport orders followed: RMLs came to Northfleet for this route just over two years later.
Bruce Jenkins

The Dartford–Purfleet Thames Tunnel is prohibited territory for cyclists. When first opened, the link was predicted to be well used by cyclists and it had been proposed to use articulated vehicles to take them through the tunnel – but the Tunnel Committee was having none of that. So the six special vehicles owned by the Dartford Tunnel Joint Committee were operated by LT, in whose highly standardised scheme they failed to fit. Thames was the brand name at the time for Ford commercial road vehicles, Trader was the model name; thus TT for the type code. The Strachans-bodied buses were reversed into special bays for loading up to 23 bicycles; they had seating for 33 passengers (in case there were any tandems) on the upper deck. Disability vehicles were not catered for. Both cycle loading and passenger boarding could be accomplished on either side, with room for tricycles and tandems at the rear. The absence of a door at the foot of each direct staircase would give later proponents of increased safety a worthy case. Introduced in September 1963, the buses had a short operational life on their dedicated operation, the last of them being withdrawn in October 1965 because of poor patronage and replaced by the Tunnel operator's Land Rovers working as required. *Bruce Jenkins*

Above As the 1960s progressed, operation of rear-engined double deckers was gaining ground rapidly. London, however, continued investment in its own Routemaster concept, altering it occasionally to fit a different requirement or change in the law. London Transport commissioned, very late in the day in 1964, the building of its own rear-engined design. By this time the Leyland Atlantean PDR 1 model had been in production for roundly six years, with the model having first appeared two years before that on LT's doorstep at the 1956 Earl's Court Commercial Motor Show. London Transport clearly still believed in itself to the full extent that it knew better than British vehicle manufacturers what it needed to suit London operating conditions. Though the historic link between LT and AEC – the latter now well subsumed within the ACV group – had long since been broken, it seemed there may still be lingering allegiance between operator and manufacturer to the disadvantage thus far of other mainstream chassis makers. The rear-engined Routemaster concept was kept highly confidential, not to say secret: evidence for this is suggested by two respected sources producing contradictory information concerning the numbers of sets of parts needed, varying from three to five. For either figure, only one set of parts – nearly two-thirds of which were from the standard Routemaster manual – were put together for the bus photographed in Vauxhall Bridge Road in early July 1966, a few days after entering service from Tottenham garage. Clearly in view here are the two lower deck emergency exits: one in the rear bay, the other signified by the door halving the foremost bay. These doors would prove invaluable in a future incident . . .
Barry Le Jeune

Right When built, FRM 1 had a sealed ventilating arrangement whereby air was fed into the saloons via slots above the side windows, so rendering openable windows unnecessary. On 31st August 1967, the engine caught fire. The saloons filled with smoke and fumes. Firemen smashed some windows to aid dispersal. Despatched to Chiswick works , FRM 1 had standard Routemaster openable windows inserted, seen here as the bus enters Tottenham garage. The minuscule fleet number in white characters, of similar style to the internally-applied fleet number discernible through the rear window of the entrance door, can just be made out beneath the garage code and running number stencil plate. Advertising posters had still not been affixed. *Capital Transport*

76
Stoke Newington
Bank Blackfriars
Waterloo
WESTMINSTER
KGY 4 D

Though looking rather more workmanlike than many twenty-first century London bus offerings, the plainness of the Park Royal bodywork design was spoilt by the fussy, ungrouped elements in the lower front panel. At the time, London drivers would normally drive at night with sidelights only switched on, and Atlantean XA 19's and Fleetline XF 5's look small enough as to be unnoticeable in well lit surroundings. The random placement of lights, registration number, roundel and black-framed ventilation louvres presents a lack of cohesion. The lack of a lifeguard rail served to emphasise the severe base line without curve-under or tumblehome. Both Leyland and Daimler types were on exchange trials in which the latter gave a rather better mechanical reliability than the former. Stamford Hill's architectural background also appears in a rather fussy Edwardian period style above renewed shop fronts in April 1966. *Alan Osborne, Maurice Bateman*

The red Leyland Atlantean XAs and green Daimler Fleetline XFs swapped places in their fairly brief London life and XF 7 is the vehicle seen at Stamford Hill in April 1966. *Alan Osborne*

The upper deck interior of XA 9, showing the very 'provincial' look of the windows. *J. Mackenzie*

In its eye-catching light blue and silver livery and with somewhat understated Blue Arrow insignia, Daimler Fleetline XF 8 awaits its next duty period on Blue Arrow route A2 standing at Stevenage garage on its first day of operation, 29th December 1969. London Transport legal ownership wording is applied to the lower foremost side panel but London Country fleetnames were displayed from the start in view of the takeover three days later. The service gave a fast, direct journey from Stevenage New Town's residential areas to the factories and offices in the industrial area. Regular passengers who bought a season ticket were guaranteed a seat from a boarding point near their home to a stop close to their work place, and back, in the morning, at midday for their lunchbreak, and at the end of their working day. XF 6 is seen out on the road. *Alan Osborne, John Boylett*

The AEC/Park Royal one-and-a-half deckers belonged to British European Airways, but were operated on that corporation's behalf by London Transport. They were based on the Regal mark IV chassis as used for the 15 RFWs; their bodywork carried 37 passengers split between the two levels, with all their luggage stowed beneath the rear raised part. An outwards opening door mid-way along the saloon gave entry to this purposeful design, no doubt aimed to set the tone for the ensuing relatively short flight. They came in two batches: one of 50, the other of 15, in a livery of black wings, dark grey lower panels and light grey upper, separated by a white waist band edged with polished aluminium strips containing dark carmine insets – a similar scheme to the corporation's aircraft and not nearly so fussy in appearance as the description suggests. They were garaged in Victoria's lower level, to operate from the new inner London Terminal by the Thames at Waterloo. The twin blinds show the airline and destination of the passengers aboard – Hanover in this example, in September 1965 – since the coach's complement was intended for that single flight. This one wears a subsequent livery simplified to a single shade of grey as it descends the Hammersmith flyover. *Bruce Jenkins*

An unidentified airport coach just about shows a later livery through the wet road grime after coming in to stand at Victoria railway terminus. The grey has given way to a dull blue, the band is now black and all is cheered by the scarlet BEA square motif. The early semaphore trafficators remain, however. *Barry Le Jeune*

The bus that persuaded BEA to invest in double deckers to replace the one-and-a-half deckers when the time came. An AEC Regent mark V, its Park Royal bodywork continued the principle of shallow upper deck windows and deeper lower deck ones – though the forward offside window was less deep than the two behind due to its being within the emergency door frame. The whole design looked poorly thought through, emphasised by a curious dark-coloured roof, a scarlet BEA symbol on the between-decks side panel that failed to relate to the airline fleetname, and an odd black version of the symbol placed asymmetrically to the nearside of the front blind box but not aligning with it. New in 1961, the bus carried passengers' luggage in the windowless rear part of the lower saloon; the succeeding Routemasters would convey the luggage in a special trailer. The former Hammersmith trolleybus depot housed the BEA vehicles from 1960; in May 1966 it comfortably accommodated the Regals MLL 744 and NLP 645 as well as the trial Regent. *Capital Transport*

Above right London's lonely Routemaster: a version that seemed at the time to give some chance of commercial success for its ACV group manufacturers, though was not apparently creating much excitement among the LT highest management. Before the war, LT had been as cool as many of the country's bus operators in operating front entrance double deckers – a name later amended to forward entrance when the doorway was placed ahead of the front wheels, opposite the driver – and then had operated only two modest production batches of STLs in the Country Area. RMF 1254's introduction at the 1962 Earl's Court Commercial Motor Show was a bit late in the day; and after the show it began an erratic life of occasional provincial wanderings between lengthy periods of storage. Clearly taking its cue from the RML design – the same inserted mid-way bay was used – the bus was surely intended for trials on LT service, but they never came. The service it did work in London was the BEA airline run connecting the West London Air Terminal by Gloucester Road, here, to Heathrow Airport. The sidelong advertisement clearly had an affinity with the fleetname carried by the usual vehicles on the airport run parked alongside: AEC Regal mark IV one-and-a-half deckers, which in due course would be replaced by Routemasters of the shorter length but with forward doorways. Northern General had not been one of the operators to have trialled the bus (none of those that had, ordered any) but was by now the only operator outside London to have some in service. When RMF 1254 came up as the very first Routemaster for disposal, it went to join its cousins in County Durham. *Bruce Jenkins*

Right When BEA came to ordering Routemasters for its Heathrow and Central London link, it specified vehicles of the original 27ft 6ins length capable of towing a two-wheel trailer to carry luggage. To help the driver reverse the bus with trailer attached, two mirrors were provided on each side. Though the greater length of RMF 1254 was forsaken, the forward doorway position was continued. The smart blue, black and white livery had recently been seen on BEA's Executive Express coaches based on AEC Reliance chassis and certainly found favour as the Routemaster livery. Fixed, single-pane windscreens were fitted and the heater/ventilator grille above came built as half-depth. NMY 641E waits in its prescribed area in April 1968 with driver's, passenger and luggage trailer doors all innocently open, the last revealing baggage stowed inside. *Capital Transport*

BEA BRITISH EUROPEAN AIRWAYS
All over Europe
BEA
B.E.A.
All over Europe
BEA
254 CLT
LONDON
BEA
SH EUROPEAN AIRWAYS BEA
MLL 734

BEA
BEA
BRITISH EUROPEAN AIRWAYS
BEA
NMY 641E
LOOK LEFT

SINGLE DECKERS

Though making up the majority of vehicles in nearly all overseas fleets, the single-deck bus has shared its position with the double decker in British fleets on a far more generous basis. For the first century of motor buses in London, the single decker has consistently been in the minority. By the decade under review, the smaller bus was accounting for roundly ten to 15 per cent of the bus fleet. Forward control single-deck buses, where the driver sits alongside the engine, were destined for early withdrawal, leaving a few normal control (driver behind engine) buses and just over 700 underfloor-engined vehicles. But the ratio between single- and double-deck types was planned to change in the next two decades rather more than it actually did.

To see how the operation of single-deck buses with separate doorways for entry and exit might work, London Transport arranged to acquire three AEC Reliances with Willowbrook bodywork to the same 30ft length as the majority of RFs but to 8ft width, into which were fitted 42 closely spaced seats. They were trialled from several garages, starting at Hemel Hempstead where they ran on routes 322 and 322A. The three comprised the RW type and stayed within the country bus department for their brief three years with LT, ending up back at their first garage in October 1963, immediately being despatched to Garston for storage and disposal.

In 1963, three new ideas for express road services – quite separate from Green Line – were examined and reported upon in some detail. They ultimately resulted in the Red Arrow concept of 1966. One concerned routes connecting suburban centres and avoiding central London. Though neither type of bus was mentioned in the report, reference to Green Line route 725's success as a cross-suburban express route – operated by RFs – could suggest that single deckers would be used on any routes stemming from this review. Nothing came of this idea.

A second idea listed, though almost certainly one that would have employed double deckers, was for express services to link residential areas to large centres of industry. After some soul searching, it was felt there was no scope here. However, at the very end of the decade, some seven years later, a somewhat similar scheme – the Blue Arrow – was to be tried in the country area at Stevenage with double deckers.

Third came a proposal to emulate the then recently introduced 'Blue Buses' of Paris by connecting the inner suburbs with Central London using either a Routemaster similar to the RMC coach version or a 36ft long luxury coach to carry 50 passengers comfortably. The two Paris 'Blue Buses' routes were short and did not cross the centre of the city. Oddly, since Paris was taken as the example to follow in this connection, the proposed London routes not only crossed the city's centre but hardly counted as linking from the inner suburbs when proposed to run, for example, between Croydon and North Finchley via Charing Cross Road, and Ilford and Greenford via Oxford Circus. This notion, too, came to nothing.

Then a fourth idea scraped in. It was to consider running reliable, rather than express, short distance routes serving main line railway stations. It was thought a ticket-less flat fare could be charged under the driver's watchful eye, thereby dispensing with the conductor. Though not specified, implicit was the use of single-deck buses when mention came of 60-passenger capacity, only half of them seated. Originally referred to in planning as the 'Red Line Service', the name was changed to Red Arrow before the route started operation.

At the close of 1963, a quite separate idea was requested for review: that one-man operated 50-seat single deckers could replace (crew operated) double deckers on poor revenue-earning routes. Buses built to the new maximum legal length of 36ft looked increasingly likely to be seen in

London service. At this stage, design and driving practicalities of such vehicles do not appear to have been considered beyond proposing an experiment be undertaken with just one special vehicle accommodating 25 seated and 70 standing passengers. It was to have a separate entrance and exit, and since standing passengers could legally only be carried in a lower saloon, a double-deck configuration was clearly out of the running. This leaves 95 people crammed into a two door 36ft-long single decker, a quarter of them seated. As an incidental, one other point arose from this proposal. It was that to avoid delays while passengers boarded the bus and paid the driver, the idea of kerbside ticket machines could be borne in mind. This was nearly forty years before such machines were to become commonplace in central London.

Fifteen AEC Merlins with Strachans bodies were ordered in 1965. The Merlins – remembered as the manufacturer's original choice of name for its model and perpetuated by LT for the longer version – came in two varieties: XMB and XMS for traditional one-man operation in the country area and for flat-fare one-man working in the central area, respectively. Naturally, the 'X' stood for experimental. The six XMSs were earmarked for trying out the original fourth idea outlined above: an experimental short distance 'reliable' route serving a main line station, employing a coin-in-slot fare system. Red Arrow route 500 thus began its career running between Victoria

This September 1963 drawing retained in London Transport's archives shows the rear entrance and front exit layout being considered at that time for standee single deckers in the central area.

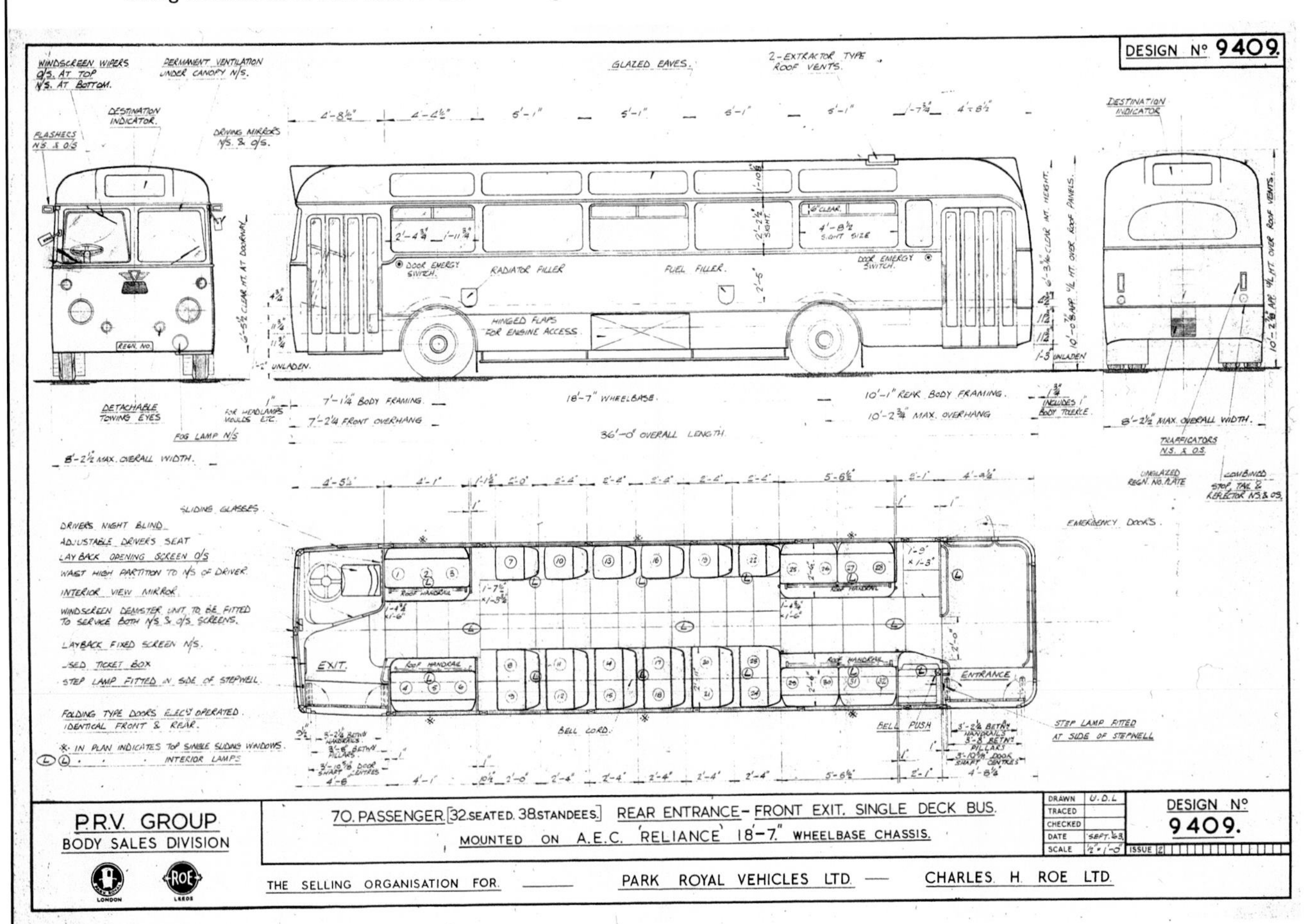

station and Marble Arch in the rush hours and extending in a loop through Mayfair back to Victoria between the morning and late afternoon peaks. There was no service on Monday to Friday evenings or at all on Saturdays and Sundays. Exceptionally, in the peak hours it carried passengers only from Victoria in the mornings and to Victoria in the evenings; in the other direction it returned empty – hopefully fast – to collect another load. After a cool start, particularly with the unfamiliar fare collection arrangement and the passengers' need to have a sixpenny piece ready to feed the coin slot (a change-giving machine apparently soon became unreliable), the experiment was deemed a success and eight of the nine Country XMBs were altered to become standee buses identical to the first six. Expansion of the Red Arrow concept had begun. Plans would be made for more such services in other parts of central London, with road conditions rather than public demand dictating the pace.

Thought had been given to the flagging Green Line operation. The RFs continued to perform reliably, but the Routemaster coaches were introduced in the belief that in replacing RFs on many routes, they would give the shot in the arm that was now very much needed. However, with reduced frequencies, the opposite proved to be the case. There were two other fronts for updating the Green Line fleet. The first, in 1965, was the introduction of 14 AEC Reliance coaches with Willowbrook 49-seat coachwork to a standard industry design, finished internally to a higher specification than the RMCs or RCLs. Their pastel grey livery with green band certainly brightened hopes for a successful introduction on the 705 which had an express section on its western arm. Regrettably, it was not to be. Living at Chiswick at the time, this author all too often came across a member of the type pulled in at the side of the Great West Road/Cromwell Road Extension with a seat cushion resting against the rear wall, the time-honoured way of indicating a broken-down vehicle.

Very much more successful was the complete rehabilitation of those Green Line RFs reckoned still to be needed for front line service once the Routemaster coaches had all been delivered. The story of the coaches' modernisation has been well rehearsed elsewhere: after the extensive work had been completed, the vehicles did look rather more contemporary with twin headlamps, curved driver's windscreen and broad light green band. Perhaps one of them could have been given the same livery treatment as the RCs, to compare how it looked, but this opportunity was not taken. The RFs so dealt with went on to give excellent, reliable service, so unlike their younger RC cousins from the same stable, whose subsequent Reliance output was far more successful.

Significantly standing out as a date in London's history of bus types and their operation is 7th September 1968, chosen as the start date of the reshaping plan. Merlins came in large number to new Red Arrow routes and to the first of many suburban 'satellite' schemes, that at Wood Green. A quantity of new buses had been stockpiled to inaugurate other flat-fare satellite schemes, the early groups identified as including Ealing, Clapham Junction, Croydon, Shepherd's Bush, Peckham and Hounslow. A round number of 150 buses was seen as being needed for these schemes and Red Arrow expansion. Early on, difficulties partly caused by the greater bulk of the MB family were quick to arise, leading to the ordering of the shorter version, the 33ft 5ins length AEC Swift. However, both versions were two and a half inches wider than RTWs and the Routemaster family, and eight and a half wider than RFs, RTs and RTLs – enough to give rise to manoeuvring difficulties when in service and storage headaches in some garages.

The Country Bus and Coach people were spared the frenetic activity of their red neighbour, with the relatively simple exercise of introducing their own version of the longer Swift, a Metro-Cammell-Weymann bodied 'Merlin' seating 45 passengers and type coded MB. Doors at both front entrance and midway exit were controlled by the driver as there was no conductor.

Towards the end of the decade, expansions of both the Red Arrow operation and the satellite routes in the suburbs were developed, requiring further single-deck buses that came in the new length. Problems arose in each case: to give as even a spread of one-man operation as possible among the garages nearest to central London, more of them were involved than might have been desired from the operational and engineering standpoints. Further satellite schemes actually implemented, for example that in the Ealing area, were not invariably concentrated on a single bus station as the introductory Wood Green one was on Turnpike Lane. This may have been because Ealing had never had a central bus station and it was unlikely that land could have been found for such a public transport facility conveniently close for main line railway and Underground interchange, even if it had been an acceptable political proposition at local level.

As the decade drew to a close, the smallest buses – Guy GS type – were being replaced by RFs redundant from other operations. Fewer than twenty of the original 84 were left in stock. These characterful vehicles with their melodious middle gears, back to front gear positions and bodywork nearly unique for London Transport, had been built by the state-owned Eastern Coach Works.

The Regal chassis had been an AEC staple since late 1929 when the London General Omnibus Co. took delivery of 50 chassis of model 662 and built suitable bodywork for them in its own Chiswick works. So began the T type. The ultimate successor, much changed, was the subcoded 15T13 version on Regal MkIII chassis model 9621E with Mann Egerton of Norwich bodywork seating 31 passengers. These final 30 members of the long lived class were always finished in the country bus livery of Lincoln green and seldom worked outside their intended territory. T 790 stands on the threshold of Tring garage in February 1962, four months before withdrawal. It illustrates the sliding door to the passenger entrance and the light coloured plate above, originally intended as background to a slotted route number stencil, long since disused. Three of the final four Ts, including this one, are recorded as being sold to a Bedfordshire scrap dealer in February 1963, the end of the line in London's country service for the half-cab single decker. *David Stevens*

The Leyland Tiger PS1 was the single-deck equivalent to that manufacturer's double-deck Titan PD1, and in the immediate post-war years of shortages of serviceable buses, London Transport was no doubt relieved to acquire 131 of the single deckers to complement the 65 double deckers added to the STD class. The first batch of TDs with Weymann 33-seat bodywork arrived at Muswell Hill garage towards the end of 1946, followed by a near two-year gap before the likes of TD 105 supplemented them. The later batch of TDs lasted in service until 1962 at Kingston (215/A) and Edgware (240A). Edgware garage's bus emerges from the short gloom of Mill Hill's railway bridges in the days before the M1 motorway extension was totally to change this area of Mill Hill Broadway. *Fred Ivey*

Below Inside a Mann Egerton-bodied TD ready for service after dark with driver's concertina blind lowered and rectangular peep hole evident. LT's typical naked lamp bulbs and surrounds imparted a certain ambience. Other features include the single seat opposite the open entrance to achieve a seating capacity of 30, and the time-honoured bell cord suspended from the ceiling, this time on the offside of centre and largely previously associated with the majority of London's trolleybuses. *Tony Belton*

240A EDGWARE STN
AND
MILL HILL BROADWAY
HARP
SALMON
TD105
JXC 298

At Kingston garage, TDs remained in service on routes 215 and 215A until the last day of February 1962. Kingston had been a real stronghold of the type in the 1950s. RFs fully took over on these services from 1st March; they had been used on the routes on Sundays since February 1960. TD 128 is seen in Esher. *Geoff Morant*

Left The driver of TD 89 has set his trafficator to flash right as he passes beneath Mill Hill railway bridges – the reason for single deckers being employed on the route. The Mann Egerton bodywork dating from 1948 was very similar, but not identical to, that gracing the last of the T types, the 15T13s. Apart from the omission of the sliding door at the entrance on the red 1/1TD2, one subtle difference was in the treatment of the front of the cab scuttle, the TD omitting the rectangular ventilator flap, and with lower set sidelights and wider spaced headlamps than the T. Starting in August 1959, when 37 buses departed the fleet, most TDs were shipped to Sri Lanka (Ceylon) for intended further service. However, TD 89 moved only a few miles south, being recorded as sold to a new owner in Willesden. *Fred Ivey*

Above The rising rear profile of the Mann Egerton body produced a dated look which at least gave space for a standard size rear advertisement. It is likely that LT would have preferred a design with the emergency door central in the back wall as had been customary, but at least in this bodywork, an extra seat was gained. The emergency way out was provided in the offside sixth bay. Not that the Mann Egertons were the final LT buses with this older style, for three provincial style Willowbrook-bodied AEC Reliances (RW type) came into experimental stock in 1960, re-introducing a similar rear end design. The vertical amber trafficators and circular red reflectors were subsequent neat additions required by a change in the law. Two pounds ten shillings was the price of a return ticket by coach from Victoria to Newcastle as advertised on TD 100's cant side. 'Lazy' blinds were available for both the route's full extent, as here, and for short workings as in preceding photographs. The design of the bus stop post seemed to underscore the confident solidity and dependability of LT generally at this time – though such impressions were to become misplaced when a certain lack of direction became apparent later in our period. *Fred Ivey*

GS 58 stands almost alone on the open parking area at Northfleet garage with only a couple of RFs for company. Introduced in 1953, the Guys, with their 26 seats, were a little larger than the 20-seat 1935–36 Leyland Cubs they replaced. Unlike the Cubs, the GS type was not allocated to Central buses, and use in the country area was to be for a shorter period, first withdrawals taking place in less than eight years. Northfleet garage – strictly speaking at Rosherville – was opened as new-built premises in the 1937 summer, with space under cover for 85 vehicles. *Howard Butler*

Above right A lone passenger leans against the shelter support at a numbered Gravesend bus stop, resigned to wait for GS 46's driver to come and open the door, where the fare can be taken for the westbound back roads route 450 journey towards Dartford. The Briggs Motor Bodies bonnet and front wings assembly were the same as those used on Thames (Fordson/Ford) lorries at the time. The compact Perkins oil engine produced a distinctive 'diesel knock' sound even when working normally, and when coupled with the Guy's melodious gearbox – whose gear selector positions were back to front compared with those on other makes – resulted in a most distinctive symphony, finished off by a rasping exhaust. *Barry Le Jeune*

Right In the early 1960s when the Country Bus Department still operated the 448 pair of routes, GSs 26 and 35 await their passengers for the journeys south eastward, while a third bus of the same type can be seen through the shelter. Both buses were transferred away from Guildford garage in autumn 1964 (GS 26 to Dunton Green, 35 to Windsor) after Tillingbourne Valley Services took over operation of these routes out of Onslow Street bus station in August 1964 – with GSs bought from LT. The front bumpers would have been chromium plated when the buses were new in 1953, but were often later painted to disguise the discolouration at their mounting points, seen best on GS 26 midway between registration number plate and foglamp. Then the paint flaked away . . . *Barry Le Jeune*

HIGH CROSS
450 SOUTHFLEET STN
GRAVESEND
BUS STOP
LONDON TRANSPORT
GS 46
MXX 346

448A PEWLEY WAY
AND
BUS STATION
GS26
MXX 326
448 GOMSHALL
NEWLANDS CORNER
PEASLAKE
MXX 335

No passport needed for this Holland! In February 1961's miserable weather, the premier Guy Special lends period atmosphere to Westerham in running as duty Chelsham 18 on the shared 464 and 465 routes. *David Stevens*

Left The GSs seemed particularly at home in rural settings. GS 55 waits at a bus stop in Knockholt while the photographer records the scene in October 1966. *Gerald Daniels*

Above right The drab environment of Harlow Bus Station emphasises the cold feeling of passengers, patiently buttoned up at 'Boarding Point 1' to pay the driver of GS 14 which itself seems to be trying to keep warm by the application of a newspaper radiator muff. The 380 route number had previously been used in the Grays area, but was re-used in the early 1960s for a cross-Harlow service linking Hertford with Sawbridgeworth. *Capital Transport*

Right Sister GS 15 is parked at Rickmansworth station stand awaiting a further tour of duty to the next-but-one Metropolitan line station towards London at Northwood. Garston garage's little bus has now been fitted with flashing trafficators at the clearly-seen high level and retains a chromed bumper, but the wheel rings and radiator outline have now been painted over. However, the well-proportioned Eastern Coach Works body looks well cared for by its home garage. *Capital Transport*

380 WARE GILSTON
HARLOW BUS STN
SAWBRIDGEWORTH
BOARDING POINT
1
GS14
MXX 314
HEATH & HEATHER

NORTHWOOD STN
309A Rickmansworth
LONDON TRANSPORT
GS15
MXX 315

Properly dressed RF 522 stands ready for a southwestward journey from Hounslow's yet to be roofed bus station. The water can, lower right, would have been rather more needed to top up radiators on route 237's predecessor buses, the three-axle LT single deckers. Prior to a rather complicated renumbering exercise in 1956, this bus had been delivered new to Dalston garage in October 1952. The legend 'PAY AS YOU ENTER' below the post-mounted display panel is repeated in the orange-coloured moulded plastic slipboard beneath the nearside windscreen, necessary upon the route's change to one-man operation in January 1965, the month in which RF 523 had come to Hounslow from Kingston garage. *Capital Transport*

Upper right Morden's bus and coach stop identity M handles passengers for a route 80A journey by RF 382. The lower case lettering introduced for route point listings was thought to be more easily read then capitals: a moot point when capitals are reasonably letterspaced, as on the 237 blind, above. Sutton garage routes 80 and 80A were changed to one-man RF operation in March 1969. *Capital Transport*

Right By May 1967, route 447 had been changed to one-man operation, having been one of the last remaining country area routes still to employ conductors. With green liveried RFs in short supply, Reigate garage has borrowed RF 387 here passing the settlement that's grown over time on Wray Common, including the tower windmill, on its way back to Redhill. *Alan Osborne*

WALTON-ON-THE-HILL
80A Sutton Belmont
LONDON TRANSPORT
RF 382
MXX 24

447

Two generations of lowbridge double deckers had worked country bus route 336, Watford–Chesham, Nashleigh Arms, till the autumn of 1965, when one-man RFs supplanted the RLHs. First, red central bus RFs were used as there were not enough green ones available; however, some time later, RF 290 came in for the Amersham garage duty. The irony is: this RF had been red when new, having been one of six (RF 289-294) to have saloon heating installed, seating reduced by one (though at 40 this was still one more than the standard RF coach) and driver operated doors to enclose the entrance. Thus modified, the six went to bolster the coach fleet, though they failed to gain any other customary Green Line touches of superiority. Among several others, RF 290 was used by British European Airways for just under a year in the mid 1960s on the airline's 'Executive Express' link for domestic flights only from the West London Air Terminal direct to airside at London Airport (Heathrow) as it was then termed. Later used on routine country bus work, previous Green Line use is betrayed by the specially designed mountings in the cant to hold the services' route legend boards. *Capital Transport*

Green Line RF 238 was among a first batch of 31 coaches to be converted to one-man operated country buses in autumn 1965. Internal comfort of deeper seating, overhead parcels racks and so on was retained, hopefully appreciated by those riding on the former coach as it turns left in the Hicks Farm Estate on urban High Wycombe's hilly pan-handle route 442. Externally, the Green Line route board mountings in the cant were completely removed, barely detectable rivet patches remaining, unlike RF 290 above. *Capital Transport*

The lengthy and meandering route 390 provided work for RF 644, here having crossed the overhead electrified Cambridge to Liverpool Street railway line at Roydon station. The bus is about to mount the slight hump of the River Stort bridge, before reversing its direction across Harlow and heading northward to reach its displayed destination. The sturdy Metro-Cammell bodywork would scarcely have noticed the uneven level crossing. *Barry Le Jeune*

Luton garage's Green Line RF 89 takes passengers on board in its Bedfordshire home town for the ride beyond the car factories and northeastward into Hertfordshire's narrow lanes at Cockernhoe on the twisty ride to Hitchin. Luton Corporation's Leyland Titan PD2 with Midland Red style built up bonnet collects passengers at the rear for the shorter suburban journey to Stopsley. *Barry Le Jeune*

Ready for the 437 version of the several routes that connected Addlestone with Woking in July 1966, RF 604 demonstrates the well remembered single-manned appearance of this classic type. With bodywork designed by LT and made by Birmingham based Metro-Cammell to be best suited for London service in the 1950s, their build quality was so good that they easily outlasted their intended life span. Many achieved well over twenty years – towards a million miles – in front line service. The supplementary PAY AS YOU ENTER notice in green lettering alongside the running number exhorts 'Fares ready please'. The picture suitably portrays the quiet ambience of a suburban country garage with trees shading a Routemaster coach and temporary bus stop signs. The garage's external lamps (above the rear of the RF) were of a design in use by the LGOC elsewhere by 1932. No longer needed at the end of the century, Addlestone garage, which could have solved the ensuing problem faced by nearby Cobham Bus Museum of having to find alternative premises, was instead demolished in 1998 and replaced by housing. *Capital Transport*

Above right It's early September 1961 and Wood Street beholds this unusual sight. In front, green RF 551 stands fully dressed for red bus service out of not-too-distant Kingston garage, even to the appropriate poster having been applied to the cant curve, the same as the third bus in line: a lingering TD with Mann Egerton body working out the end of its London life. In those days, Bentall's, the well known department store, ran a petrol station and car garage, in view behind the three RFs and TD. *David Stevens*

Right Delivered new in Festival of Britain year 1951 for private hire and tourist excursion work, RF 22 stands a little worse for wear after later Green Line duty, for which the front blind box had been partly masked to accommodate restricted details. The coach had been the emergency substitute vehicle at Victoria and so needed to display any of the destinations with route number in the network. The venetian blinds, now broken, are unlikely to have been used in its recent guise, as a driver training bus from Fulwell garage. *Hugh Taylor*

BENTALLS
GARAGE
KINGSTON
219 HERSHAM
ESHER
NLE 551

GREEN LINE
RF 22
LUC 222
JXC 294
JXC 282

RF 309 was one of sixteen RFs to have been re-liveried in shades of green rather lighter than the traditional Lincoln with light relief in the 1960 summer. A year later, the coach which had been adapted from green bus use and renumbered from RF 528, stands on the slope outside Reigate shed displaying this brighter livery with black embellishments on the wheels, rather dirty here after the run from the home garage at High Wycombe. *David Stevens*

Occupying the space labelled by British Railways as 'Bus Stand Only', RF 180 rests in rustic Berkshire after an arduous journey from Kentish Thames-side on the Green Line 702. Northfleet's coach displays the unnumbered route board suitable for RFs on either 701 or 702. The sideways-on bus and coach stop flag was so positioned to be seen from the street. Its unusual, if not unique, setting right by the stopblock of a railway siding would hardly be found today, but this was Sunningdale station in May 1966. As an aside, no LT bus route came to this stop: the major operators serving this area of thin traffic were Thames Valley and Aldershot & District. *Alan Osborne*

A few passengers alight from RF 174 on arrival in Buckingham Palace Road, Victoria from Gravesend – and no-one looks set to board the empty coach for its continued westbound journey to Sunningdale. Starting in summer 1966, 174 vehicles were refurbished in this way (RF 136 had been the 'modernised' forerunner) in a programme undertaken at Aldenham works. Taking eleven months to complete, there were then enough Modernised RFs to meet the single-deck Green Line scheduled duties. The cant level route board, still 14ft 3in long and 7in deep, is now in black lettering on a yellow ground, similar to that used on the RC coaches when introduced in the previous November. *Capital Transport*

RF 131 is seen away by an inspector from Golders Green bus station's stop B. Green Line Express route 727 was introduced in November 1964 to take advantage of the London extension of the M1 motorway in linking Tring with Hemel Hempstead, Mill Hill and Victoria on weekdays. The driver's signalling window is open enough for ventilation, while the offside trafficator flashes right in confirmation of departure. A well driven Green Line RF gliding gently along undulating roads could produce an almost soporific effect for the comfortably seated passenger – the most pleasant of stage travel in the period. *Capital Transport*

In spring 1968, consequent upon a reduced need for RFs on Green Line work, RF 104 was one of 25 modernised coaches to be used as country buses, the outward differentiation being limited to repainting the light green band to yellow and a new LONDON TRANSPORT bullseye design central on the front panel. 'Before and after' are clear to see at the bus station in front of Dorking garage on either side of RT 622. Coach RF 35 stands to the right, set to depart for Dunstable on route 713 which had been changed to one-man operation in February 1969. The conveniently sited premises here were closed in 1990, demolished and replaced by housing. *Barry Le Jeune*

Introduced just in time for the Festival of Britain celebrations in May 1951, the RFWs were intended for use on prestigious or longer distance hirings. The AEC Regal mark IV chassis was the standard product, less altered than the RF for LT's needs, and fitted with the 8ft wide Eastern Coach Works body, which together gave a rather more comfortable ride than outward appearance suggests. At this time when, with the newly relaxed permitted length of 30ft and the underfloor engine concept in full flow, coachwork suppliers were generally very busy, building somewhat more glamorous designs than this product of the Lowestoft factory. LT took 15 of the twenty built. RFW 14 loads outside Charing Cross Underground station, now Embankment after its street namesake. The outward opening hinged passenger door remains a novelty for a London Transport bus or coach. *Howard Butler*

Rather than try to divide the LT motif transfer to sit comfortably central in the width of the luggage boot doors, it was instead displayed at the foot of the rear window, just within the range of the seat headrests – a rare treat on any London Transport vehicle. The four tail lamps on RFW 1 are originals, while the circular red reflectors are additions made to all LT buses and coaches to comply with a change in law. *Howard Butler*

As they were intended for private hire use, the RFWs had no destination equipment when built. Demonstrating another use, RFW 4 leaves Victoria coach station with the small top nearside windscreen strip showing a neat, if scarcely noticeable, announcement that it is intent on carrying passengers on a 'Windsor & Hampton Court Tour'. Much glass allowed full sightseeing views; indeed, with glass valences too – a rare hangover from prewar 'luxury' coach design – any passenger overheating through such an amplitude of glass could lower his window within the depth of the valence to achieve (in theory, at least) some draughtless ventilation. *Howard Butler*

Most RFWs were sold out of London service to the Ceylon Transport Board, later Sri Lanka. RFWs 6 and 14 however stayed close to home, finding new ownership at the start of 1965 with Harling of Waterloo, SE1, on staff transport duties for St Thomas' Hospital. RFW 14, now equipped with circular flashing trafficators at sidelamp height, quietly heads along Broad Sanctuary past Westminster Abbey in May 1969. Both RFWs later entered preservation. *Barry Le Jeune*

The last of three AEC Reliance buses, RW 3, is posed at Reigate garage as though for service in a publicity view soon after delivery (*above*). None of the three worked from this garage. Later, in service, RW 1 stands ignored by two ladies at the southbound bus stop opposite St Albans garage. The main point of the RW trio, the first two of which were delivered in September 1960 for staff training on routes 322/A, was to see how well single manning with a separate entrance from exit worked. This trial was conducted in the country area only, at three Hertfordshire garages (Hemel Hempstead, St Albans and Hertford) and one in Surrey (Addlestone). The otherwise well rounded Willowbrook body was spoiled by a bland front end design hardly improved by emphasising the fixed, raked driver's windscreen by a brightwork frame. The shallow indicator box looks like an afterthought: the route points are in a smaller size lower case lettering to fit within the restricted space. *David Stevens, Colin Brown*

An altogether different vehicle from the RW bus was the RC coach – yet by its pedigree, it could be regarded as a successor from the same stable. Whereas the RW was a modest sized AEC Reliance similar in dimensions to its Regal mark IV RF predecessor apart from increased width to 8ft, the RC was a full blown Reliance 2½in wider still and 6ft longer at 36ft. The earlier AH 470 7.7 litre engine was now superseded by the AH 690 11.3 litre unit to power the 49-seat bodywork, also built by Willowbrook to an operator-group standard design both distinctive and pleasing. RC 10 collects passengers on Eccleston Bridge, Victoria, for the announced Limited Stop run via Cromwell Road Extension on Green Line route 705 to Windsor in January 1966. The coach is finished in its newly introduced livery of pastel grey and green, seen by some to be a lighter shade than the traditional Lincoln variety. When the express sections (Colnbrook by-pass and Chiswick flyover/Great West Road extension to Hammersmith) were introduced on 28th August 1963, crews were instructed to display blue background Express blinds on the Victoria–Windsor stretch. The express version was withdrawn in December 1967.

The 14 RC coaches soon failed to live up to their expectations through mechanical unreliability. By the end of 1967 they had been removed from the prestigious 705 run and many saw no service till re-introduction in the following May on Green Line Express route 727, as Reigate's RC 1 shows here at Heathrow Airport bus station, bound for Luton. The coach has been altered for single manning and has luggage carrying capacity installed behind the driver – the protective brightwork cages can be seen occupying the first bay. Seating has been reduced from 49 to 43 accordingly. The coach, laden with passengers, stood a less than average chance of completing its journey, for those vehicles that were put back into service (all in the changed livery) were withdrawn for a second time, again owing to their propensity to fail. *Malcolm Young*

Top A new concept introduced in April 1966 was the Red Arrow service in the core of London: close headway, short routes intended to move large numbers of passengers relatively short distances for a flat fare. As an experiment to start with, six Strachans-bodied AEC Swifts of the 36ft-long P2R type that LT called after the manufacturer's early choice of model name – Merlin – entered service on route 500. The unexpected choice of body builder produced this fairly severe design with matching peaked domes fore and aft. The fixed windscreen sloped inwards vertically at the top on the driver's side in an attempt to minimise reflections. Here, XMS 5 collects passengers at Waterloo for the Red Arrow 507 service over Lambeth Bridge to Victoria which replaced that part of the route 46 not long before this September 1968 scene. *Barry Le Jeune*

Above XMB 1 had been the first in a batch of nine experimental dual-door country buses, the next eight of which were earmarked before entering service for conversion to standee layout as XMS class and repainting into red livery to bolster the successful Red Arrow operation. By the end of the decade a couple of years later, the bus had a settled life at Tring garage. It was usually to be found wending its way along the 387, connecting the pretty village of Aldbury, a popular scene in which to photograph the route's bus, via Tring station (the main passenger point) with Tring to which it here returns. *David Brown*

Alone among the first production batch of the 36ft-long Merlins was MBA 18 with its SMM-F registration. The production buses for the Red Arrow routes were bodied by the Birmingham-based MCW firm to a rather less severe look than the Strachans predecessors. Many drivers disliked the low seated driving position, with the steering wheel only just above the grey rounded instrument binnacle in clear view here at Victoria in September 1968. Red Arrow buses displayed white on blue background blinds, the LT custom for limited stop routes. *Barry Le Jeune*

The overall roof of Turnpike Lane bus station shades three Merlins on W-prefixed 'satellite' routes in August 1969. MBS 46 typifies the new generation of one-man operation buses originally built for 25 seated and 48 standing passengers, quantities unheard of in earlier London single-deck buses, even in wartime. The capacity proportion was quite soon changed to 32 seated/34 standing by adding seven single seats in the front standing area. The inspector turns to have a word with MBS 69's driver while MBS 77 awaits departure on a third short local route, W1. The flake grey relief band introduced on the XMS was reduced in depth on the production buses so it stopped short of brightening the frontal aspect, a finishing touch now left to a bright alloy strip beneath the curved matching pair of windscreens. The LT fleetname reappeared in red on the production MBS type's grey relief after having been dropped in favour of italic capitals *RED ARROW* for the dedicated XMSs. On both versions, the open roundel device was the frontal evidence of operator; only the front wheel hub covers announced the chassis manufacturer. *Malcolm Young*

An RT and a first generation mini-skirted young woman head past MBS 470 on display in Wealdstone High Street. The MCW-bodied bus was one of a batch of 177 suburban flat fare vehicles now to have a higher driving position. The dual coin-in-slot symbols were intended to indicate to boarding passengers to have coins ready to drop into the automatic ticket machines. *Barry Le Jeune*

In August 1969 routes 110 and 111 were converted to MBS to test equipment designed to handle coarsened fares. The routes were worked by ten vehicles out of Hounslow garage. Here at Cranford, a rather apprehensive-looking passenger steps into MBS 552 to encounter a fare payment method many people found hard to understand in the brief moment of boarding, despite – or perhaps due to – the many signs, one of which is the yellow strip on the front nearside panel worded "PAY AS YOU ENTER 3d 6d & 1/- pieces only please". The high level white panel to the left of the middle doors reminds "No Entry".

Turning left into Ealing Road, MB 622 is framed in the background by Alperton garage. One of only nine Merlins to be registered in the WMT-G series, it was caught working the Sundays only route 83A, a one-man operation introduced in October 1969, here in the company of an inspector. The bus was sent to a Yorkshire scrapyard in the summer of 1977 after a life of well under ten years. *Colin Brown*

The MB type came to the country area in March 1968, with driver collecting fares on route 447 out of Reigate garage; these were dual doorway entrance/exit buses intended to supersede RT and RF operations. The next Merlin country version delivered in green and yellow livery came in the following November. It was the 'standee' type two-door version typified by MBS 273 here in Reigate and came new with seats for only 25 passengers; a further 41 were expected to stand in the forward half of the bus. It could be an uncomfortable distance to a seat for the less agile passenger, particularly if the driver, in trying to keep to time, accelerated before everyone was seated after paying their fares to Autoslot machines – an unfamiliar exercise in itself. Though railway cattle trucks were compartmented to prevent animals faltering, this sobriquet was soon applied in criticism of these buses on route 430, both of whose termini are shown clearly on the indicator blind. Less readable are the route points. *Barry Le Jeune*

TAILPIECE

It was sometimes necessary, for example after minor accident damage, for garage staff to repaint registration numbers, and occasionally they made mistakes. In August 1969 RT 4353 was given the registration number NLE518 instead of NLP518, this time during repaint at Aldenham. RF 299 was the rightful owner of this registration and so a group of enthusiasts led by a driver at Seven Kings garage hired RT 4353 for a photo shoot at Grays garage, where the RF was based. The RT ran with this error for a few months, only being corrected when the photographers informed Seven Kings after their trip. *Alan Osborne*